For the Quiet

For the Quiet

ෆ෨

Abigail Grimes

A collection of poetry and prose for those
missing home
Whoever or wherever it may be

WBG/WBC PUBLICATIONS | BOWMANVILLE

Copyright © 2020 by **Abigail Grimes**

All rights reserved. No part of this publication may be reproduced, distributed or transmitted in any form or by any means, without prior written permission.

Abigail Grimes / WBG/WBC Publications
Bowmanville, ON L1C 5C4
www.abigailgrimes.com / wbgwbc.square.site

Publisher's Note: This is a work of fiction. Names, characters, places, and incidents are a product of the author's imagination. Locales and public names are sometimes used for atmospheric purposes. Any resemblance to actual people, living or dead, or to businesses, companies, events, institutions, or locales is completely coincidental.

Book Layout © 2017 BookDesignTemplates.com

For The Quiet / Abigail Grimes. -- 1st ed.
ISBN 978-1-7773863-0-6 – Paperback
ISBN 978-1-7773863-1-3 – Ebook

For Briar
A Dream

"The ache for home lives in all of us, the safe place where we can go as we are and not be questioned"

—MAYA ANGELOU

Contents

Wanting *1*
Dear Briar *2*
The Archived *3*
Ode to an Unfulfilled Uterus *5*
Empty Pocket *6*
Beloved Briar *8*
Impressions *11*
Genuine *21*
Dear Briar *23*
The Space Between *25*
Dear Briar *27*
Laugh Alone *29*
My Dearest Briar *31*
Home *32*
My Dear Sweet Briar *34*
Echoes *36*
Dimming Star *37*

The Spectre 41

Dear Briar 52

And Here We Are 54

My Dearest Briar 56

Acknowledgements 59

About the Author 61

For The Quiet

Wanting

You know me
You know what makes me tick

The musk of your cologne lingers
My head turns

The heat of your skin a tease
The closeness of your body torture

I feel you

Our eyes meet
My breath catches

Eyes cast down, my heart races
Your fingertips along the back of my hand as you pass

You are gone
And you leave me here

Wanting

Abigail Grimes

Dear Briar

I miss you today.

I miss you every day, but today there is an ache. A hollowness.

Today, in my heart and mind, I will keep you close. For company and for peace.

It's quiet here. We can just sit and watch the water lap the shore.

Yours, patiently waiting,

Me

For The Quiet

The Archived

You may be in her DMs, but I am in her archives.
She will always come back to me. I am her history, and possibly her future.
It is she, not you that keeps me alive.
And it is she, not you, that will be here when this is all said and done.
I have no issue with you, for you are temporary.
You pose no threat to me.
She is eternal, and to her, so am I.
I represent something to her that you never will.
Security.
No matter who will slide into her DMs after you, and the numerous before you,
I have always been here.
And after you are gone, she will look me up and wonder, even if just for a moment, where I am

Abigail Grimes

Long after she has forgotten your name,
    she'll still call mine out by accident
For you are but a passing fancy
I am the measure by which you and all
    others are weighed – and found wanting
I am steady and reliable; and when you're
    gone, it will be me.
It has always been me.

Ode to an Unfulfilled Uterus

Is it the lifelong goal of every woman to bring a child into this world?

I can't think that it is, that would be too unfair. It's not for everyone and for so many different reasons.

Some who can really shouldn't; and conversely, some who really should, sadly can't.

It's the luck of the draw I suppose. Not sure which card I want dealt, but it's time to play.

***

Like a broken clock running on its own schedule, you spring to life only to provide frustration and pain

Just as suddenly as you appear you are gone; leaving confusion and sadness in your wake

***

Abigail Grimes

Empty Pocket

You serve no purpose

You fill with random bits of everyday things

The remnants of something else's purpose

Collector of refuse; bits of an unfulfilled future cling to you only to be washed away

You are the empty pocket in a tattered pair of old blue jeans

Fraying and failing and held onto for no better reason than the memory of a potential use

For The Quiet

Twice repaired, stitch and ironed

It's time that you were retired

Unable to hold, to fulfill your duty,

You have not served me well.

Goodbye Pocket.

Abigail Grimes

Beloved Briar

I write you today because I now know what needs to be done and I know that means the only way I will ever talk to you is by letter.

Here, in words, on paper, we can be authentic. Ourselves. We can be together.

Out there, well, there can be no we. No us.

I thought I was prepared, but I suppose I'm not. Not truly. I guess the situation we're in is only now beginning to dawn on me. And it is harder than I thought it would be.

For The Quiet

I am plagued with guilt. Was I too weak? Did I not fight hard enough?

I need you to forgive me.

These things take time. That I understand. I hope that one day you will.

Yours. Always.

Me

Abigail Grimes

Impressions

She sat in the living room and stared out the window as the world around her woke up. The snow fell steadily that winter morning, covering roofs, cars and fence posts with a fluffy white cap. It was almost transcendent. Her mind drifted to grade school when a day like this brought with it the possibility of hearing those magic words: "Snow Day". You could go outside and make snow angels, run and play. Those days had long since passed, but the excitement remained. She gave a passing thought to what her neighbours would think if she were to go outside and make snow angels. She cared too much about what her neighbours thought.

George Michael crooned in the background. The seductive tenor of his voice slid down her spine. She didn't know why she did this to herself. No one needs slow jams on a Sunday morning. Her wedding song played next. It threatened to carve a hole in her gut, but she didn't turn it off. She must be a glutton for punishment.

She closed her lips. The sound of her voice echoed mournfully in the cavernous space. She was aware that she talked to herself more nowadays. She couldn't remember a time when she would carry on entire conversations with herself before this. She sometimes worried that she was losing touch, but she rationalized it. Sometimes she just needed to hear things out loud. It helped her make better decisions. It helped her be more honest about seeing the different sides of a position. The truth was not nearly as complex. It was quite simple really.

She spent most of her time alone and this was how she coped.

She rushed around the house to gather and sort the laundry. There was always so much laundry. For a home with virtually only one person in it, it always seemed to need tidying.

She felt as though she were being haunted. A ghost lived in her house. It was unnerving at times, but if she were honest, she would say that it was also comforting. Those were the times when just knowing that she wasn't completely alone was enough.

She hadn't laid eyes on him in weeks. Her ghost. But she knew he was around. There were always signs. A shoe left askew, a new dish in the sink. And the one sign that haunted her the most. The fog on the bathroom mirror, the dampness in the air and the steady hum of the fan. When that was the case she knew she had just missed him.

She missed him.

She spent most of her time alone. It bred an unsettled ache in her chest, a churn in her gut, a persistent tear that threatened to spill down her cheek.

Abigail Grimes

She hadn't signed up for this, but it was routine now.

One week he slept upstairs, so as not to disturb her. Another week, he slept upstairs because it was darker during the day.

He slept upstairs.

She thought he would have been awake when she got up. It was seven in the morning and there was no sign of him. The thought of climbing the stairs to peek in seemed, somehow, intrusive. Like a mother with a teenaged child. He will come down when he's ready, she thought. There were things to do, errands to run, and today she would do them alone. She did them alone most of the time.

They were strangers. That was just the reality of the thing.

She glanced at the clock on the mantle. A gift from a time long passed. The small gears toiled and the sound drew her attention. She came to realize how quiet the house was. The deafening squeal of the tiny gears forced her out of the chair.

Just leave the room.

She stood, suddenly feeling foolish. Was this how other people were in their own homes? That question again. What do the neighbours do? Who cares? She did.

Her footfalls mocked her as she walked to the kitchen. *Slap, slap, slap,* the sound of her size 10 feet on the engineered hardwood. Even the hardwood was engineered. Contrived. Like the string of vague thoughts that shuffled in her mind – like a deck of cards. A deck comprised entirely of Jokers.

She just wanted something to eat. It was not all she wanted, but she would have to make due for now. With the thought of a balanced breakfast, like one you would see on television, she opened the door and came face to face with an empty fridge.

A testament to her loyalty.

Her foolishness.

The knowledge that there were things that needed to be done out-weighed all else. They needed groceries, they needed paper towels. There were errands to run, and going weeks without supplies in an effort to ensure that they did these things together, no longer made sense.

Had it ever made sense?

She showered and dressed in weekend warrior gear. A pair of yoga pants, tank-top, t-shirt and a hoodie. Layers. It was winter after all. She pulled on her medium cold-weather coat and boots and called out to him, to advise she was going out for a little while.

She received no response. She was not surprised.

In the garage sat his car, his baby. Not having one of flesh and blood, this was the closest thing to fill that void. She hated the thing. She was almost positive that he loved it more than he loved her. They had been together just as long.

Hitting the open road, even if it was to run silly errands, always freed her. She felt in control of her own destiny when she was in her car. Once on the highway, she sped along with the flow of traffic and turned the music up. Way up. She sung out loud. Unabashed. Free. She sung desperate love songs, rock songs and show tunes. The ghost did not inhabit her car. It could not haunt her here. It was tethered to the house.

But then, Guilt. Guilt often accompanied Free. It was Free's little brother who was always hiding just out of sight. Ready to tell. Always ready to cause trouble. And there it sat, in the shopping cart, ready to throw a fit.

Why couldn't you just wait? You were supposed to do this together. Guilt's whine escalated. It was a sound so powerful, so overwhelming, that even though she tried, it would not be ignored. It was a sound only she could hear.

She finished up the errands and headed home. She wanted to be home when he finally appeared. She wanted to see him. Touch him. Talk to him. Face to face.

The heaviness of the apparition closed around her as she pulled her car into the driveway; but it wasn't until she pulled into the garage that she realized her miscalculation. His vehicle was gone. This was not the weekend she thought it was.

She would not see him. Not today.

She sat in the car. The moment of grief intense, but it would pass. It always did. The upholstery of her car had absorbed more than its fair share of tears over the years. What was one or two more?

She blew out an angry, saddened breath and got out of the vehicle. She hauled the heavy grocery bags into the house. At least she wouldn't go hungry while she finished the laundry and cleaned.

There were new dishes in the sink. He must have arisen moments after she left. Or, who knows, maybe he had been awake the whole time. Lying in wait until she had gone. Waiting until it was safe to haunt the grounds freely.

It had stopped snowing and the hours whiled away.

She debated the tenets of global warming, fad dieting and marriage. That was a touchy one. It usually left her red in the face and emotionally drained, feeling as though her body had been turned inside out, her nerves exposed.

It would be three days of this.

Bearing down, she made her peace with it. She had no other choice.

Work, home. Work and home.

The shadows drew longer. They inched along the walls and slid across the floorboards, reaching for her.

One more wretched echo would have broken her, but the pillows were back on the bed.

The apparition made tangible. They were free to talk, to touch, to be together. But nothing was ever that easy. It would take some time to get used to sharing the bed again.

The gears of the clock turned loudly. They hadn't much time.

In three days the cycle begins anew.

Abigail Grimes

For The Quiet

Genuine

It was all Fake
Everything
It was a Front – It was a Ruse
It's True
All this time you spend building this thing –
you have been Lying
How hollowing to see it for the first time
It's a Lie
What happens now?
Plan B was always Plan A
Where is the Path?
How do you find You – when you have been
so lost for so long?
How do know what's right when you
thought you were right all along?
The time is Now
It is now time to Live

Abigail Grimes

> *To Be True*
> *To live for maybe the first time,*
> *Honestly,*
> *Your Genuine Life*

For The Quiet

Dear Briar

It's raining again today and it mirrors how my heart aches.

I could not get you off my mind this weekend. Nothing could distract me. And I tried. I really did. I tried to watch television, to sleep. I even tended the garden.

But you were there. In everything.

Every bloom, every character. Every dream.

You are a dream.

Abigail Grimes

I write to you to say that though, at times, I may feel haunted by you, I don't know any other way to be. And I don't think I could exist without your shadow near me.

Missing you everyday,

Me

The Space Between

The air is still
There is no sound
All that exists is this

There is electricity in the space
*   between moments*
Between molecules of light and dark
Between us

The craving. The pulse. The mystery.
It ends here
Now

The moment draws near
Familiar, yet distant
A memory

Breath warms my lips
And Fire ignites where your lips graze
*   mine*

Abigail Grimes

The sensation too sweet to last

I have longed for this
To remember
To feel

Tastes linger and the quiet buzz
    excites
But between breaths we know
The flames will consume if we don't
    turn away

Now but a haunting memory
It is all that can be
For the space between is vast

For The Quiet

Dear Briar

It is no surprise that I can't stop thinking of you.

The culmination of recent events leads me down a road where you are at the end

But you are not there.

You are a ghost.

I feel haunted by you

I want you to let me go; yet I am unwilling to know the world without you in it.

Everything this week reminded me of you

The Spectre of you hangs around my shoulders

And yet there is nothing more comforting than conjuring you in my mind's eye

Abigail Grimes

> You bring me back to myself
>
> You ground me
>
> You remind me what love is, for you are love
>
> I will never get to touch you, to feel you in my arms.
>
> To brush away your tears or hear the tinkle of your laugh
>
> But I feel you in me
>
> And while it hurts, I will endure the pain
>
> Because it brings me closer to you
>
> I won't forget you
>
> In the stillness of the night, I am heartbroken
>
> But I am grateful
>
> Rest, Beloved.
>
> Rest

For The Quiet

Laugh Alone

I Laugh, Alone

Do you remember when
    Dot dot dot

I fill in the blanks
    Left to laugh alone

The smile on my face is for both of us
    But only I understand its sadness
        Yours is a plastic smile
        A mask

It cuts deep to see you try
    Even deeper when you don't

A shrug
    Dismissed in a moment

Abigail Grimes

> *Cut to the quick*
> > *But who do I tell?*
> > > *Who will remember?*

There is only one thing to do
> *And to it, I heartily subscribe*

I will laugh.
> *Alone.*
> > *For both of us.*

My Dearest Briar

I'm sitting on a train this morning, thinking about you.

I'm always thinking of you.

It's raining here. I often wonder what it is like where you are. Does it rain?

I would imagine if it does, the most beautiful gardens would bloom.

Here, without you, the grey skies darken and a storm threatens.

I will take shelter from the elements and when the sun breaks through, I will take those tears from heaven and plant a garden in honour of you.

Yours Faithfully,

Me

Abigail Grimes

Home

It was a misty morning in May when I drove down the street in the same dingy town I had grown to love,

And to hate.

That's how it was, more often than not, with hometowns, wasn't it?

The same roads, same houses, but today, one stood out more than the others.

The washed out blue and white paint on the porch had been worn away by rain and neglect.

The roof over the rusted screen door dipped and yawned, its shingles twisted and raised.

In the window hung an unlighted ornament in the shape of a Christmas tree.

For The Quiet

Was it unplugged? Or had a bulb simply blown?

Snow had long since gone from this place as had any whisperings of holiday cheer.

I wondered how long it would remain there, and if anyone inside even looked out that window anymore.

The scant front lawn was unkempt. A mower had not touched it all season, and perhaps, not even the season before.

It was the very vision of disrepair.

But somehow, reaching out from the tangled mess, was a pale and yellow daffodil.

And in this place, just like that town,

My home,

Hope still lived there.

My Dear Sweet Briar

Lately, I can't seem to get you off my mind. I have been dreaming of you.

Bittersweet dreams.

Dreams that, at times, drape around my shoulders like a thick blanket. Warm and heavy, I find them comforting.

It is in those times that I forget.

I forget what it took to be where I am today. I forget about the choices I made that deliberately, purposefully, took you from my arms.

It has been difficult to come to terms with those choices and every time I am convinced that I have, you somehow appear and I am broken again.

I know that what I have done was the right thing to do. Knowing that, and living with the choice, are very different.

I tried, I truly did.
Writing these letters to you is all I can do and I hope they eventually find you. For, now, that is all I can do.

Time passes so quickly and right now, it seems that all I can do is breathe.

I have to find my way.

But I know that you will always be with me. In my heart and in my soul.

Love you always,

Me

Abigail Grimes

Echoes

The way you say her name,
    It's like an apology

    To whom are you sorry?
        Her? Me?

    I don't need your apologies,
    I've had years to reconcile

    Still, the truth clangs
    Harsh echoes in my mind.

        When I feel your breath, soft on my neck,
    Your arms wrapped tight around me,

    I wonder,
Is it my turn to apologize?

Dimming Star

*How long can a galaxy last once its star
has burnt out?*

Once the star burns out there is nothing

Nothing but the cold, empty void of space

And everything in its sphere dies

Do we know how long it takes?

Before the message gets through

*Before you know for certain that no one is
coming for you?*

*What do you do in that horrible expanse
of time?*

Do you knit or sew?

Abigail Grimes

Do you sing?

Random aching words that no longer have meaning?

Or do you stir, aimless, haunted

Until all is still

Until there is no more

You will wait. You are gallant and brave.

Hopeful.

Foolish.

And as ice forms and breathing becomes more laboured,

What might before have passed for a thought drifts by

You should have left

For The Quiet

*Now, with unblinking eyes frozen in
resolve and despair*

You watch

As the world ends

Abigail Grimes

The Spectre

The Spectre hung over us for too long and there were only so many times you could feign looking on the bright side of things before it was truly nauseating.

She hadn't eaten in over a week. She looked so frail. What were we going to do if the news was bad? What would *she* do? I don't ever remember being so worried.

Only so many times you could smile before it finally wore on you. I don't know how people do it. How the people who are going through it deal with it. You can see it, how the Spectre hangs over them, never too far from their heels. It is the very shadow beneath their eyes.

All of the appointments, the doctors, the nurses, surgeons, orderlies, admin staff. The list went on and on.

Abigail Grimes

She did such a good job protecting us. It was her job after all. She was our mom. She loved us. But she did such a great job that in the end, it proved to be a detriment. We didn't have the stuff. We could not cope.

That was a problem in a number of different areas. Money, relationships, death. The big things.

I remember attending my great aunt's funeral. I was about 16 when she passed away, and as a first generation Canadian, there weren't very many members of my family in Canada. This woman was like my grandmother. As much as my mother would allow anyway.

She was a lovely woman. She lived in a small townhouse in the city and she always smelled faintly of mothballs. I loved her and when she died I had my first brush with real heartbreak. She used to sing a song that brought us such joy as kids, so much so, that we revisit the song, and her famed dance moves, every time we get together for family dinners. She had a killer sense of humour and incredible warmth. Exactly what I thought a grandmother would be like.

My own grandmothers lived a continent away and we did not get the opportunity to visit very often. I was saddened by that fact, and when they passed I felt a loss, but not the same kind of loss. Acknowledging the difference brought with it a fair amount of guilt.

As a family we didn't talk about these things. I wouldn't even have known how to broach the topic.

When the strange behaviour started it was a long time before anyone looked into what was actually happening. My mind went to terrifying places. But I went there alone.

The strange pains, the aches, the fainting. The Fear. And everyone sat alone with their fears because none of us dared to give the Fear power.

We didn't have to. The silence did that.

The highs and lows of that year were too many to count. The first real slip was the referral for the blood test. It's supposed to be the preeminent test available. It detects it 99% of the time. But we didn't deal in the 99%. We lived in the Fear, and the Fear's realm was in the 1%. So there we stayed. For months.

Arguably, we never left.

The test came back negative. A reprieve, absolutely, but the Spectre still hung over us as a family. And with so few of us here, we have always been of the view that it is just us. We are each other's support. We were taught to look to the insular solution, because to search outward is a search in vain. No one knows what we are going through. And more than that, it's no one else's business. To let someone else in is a betrayal. And I can admit that feeling that way is a terrible strain, but I don't know any other way. I wasn't taught any other way.

The problem with that way of thinking is that when it is your mother, your teacher, who is incapacitated with Fear, there is no one. You are alone. But you do your best because you have no other choice.

The test was negative, but the symptoms persisted, and the Spectre continued to haunt. It had taken up residence in each of our houses. And like the unwelcome visitor it was, it took things from us.

First ease, then our appetites, and finally sleep.

And without sleep we slowly began to turn on one another. Stones were recklessly thrown. It is funny how you feel immune to consequence when you lob stones at family. They will always be there. Our solemn hope says yes, at a time when hope is already stretched to its limit.

The strain of the unknown was becoming more than any of us could have anticipated.

More tests. More non-answers. More frustration. Ever present Fear.

Until one day, the referral to the surgeon. And then the discussion of the will kit. I couldn't decide which one terrified me more. No, that's a lie. It was the will kit. She had never wanted to talk about it before and if she wanted to now, it meant that she was slipping further from us. The Spectre's song, a pied piper, lulling her closer to the edge of a frightening abyss.

I watched, helpless. Afraid. She was so strong. The strongest among us. How could she be so easily convinced to follow?

My fears were no longer important. The job now was to make sure, no matter what, she had all the support she needed. I would take care of me later.

There is a mass and it needs to come out. Merely a sentence. But then why did it hang there? Heavy, like sopping wet clothes on the line. It was only a sentence. Was it a death sentence?

More appointments. More scary words. And light in her eyes dimmed more. She aged so rapidly that summer as she fought the Spectre. The Fear. It lived there with her. It stood behind her and the weight of its shadow stooped her shoulders.

I had never watched someone grapple with their own mortality before. We all would like to think that we would be brave. Secure in the knowledge of a life well lived.

I was a good person. I was kind.

These are the things we say to secure ourselves against that Great Unknown. That is what we would like to think.

Truthfully, we are terrified.

Will it hurt? Will it be sudden? Will I have time to say all that needs to be said?

Vague concepts pale in the face of the Fear.

Those on the outside have our own fears. *Can I do this without her?* I was afraid of the answer, because no matter what it was, the fact remained; I had no choice.

She underwent the surgery and we all piled into our cars to make the three-hour journey to the university town where the surgeon performed nightly and taught by day. Her students, lovely little chopping machines, modeled after their idol, worked tirelessly to help remove the mass and set our universe right again.

A kilometre away, in our finely appointed lakeview hotel rooms, sleep evaded us.

It was a difficult surgery, but we got everything. Marvelous Wizard! I wanted to cry out. Joy! Pure joy! But then came the rest and with it, the Spectre emerged from its hiding place. *We sent everything for testing. We will get back to you with the results.* It appeared that the Spectre did not want us to have any peace.

I did my best at that point to put my own disappointment aside. There would be no joy, no reprieve, until the results came in.

And then they did. Positive. How did this word come to mean the exact opposite?

Suddenly the Spectre was no longer a shadow. It had a shape and size. It had, in a matter of words, transformed. It was tangible and now, when it put its hand on you, not only did you stoop, but your blood ran cold. And in this manifestation, it chose not to place its bony hand on your shoulder. It chose instead to close its hand around your throat. And squeeze. Unrelentingly.

Her eyes became vacant. Now the insular meant to retreat to the darkest space inside yourself. She wouldn't hold your gaze for more than a moment. But in those instances when she didn't know we were watching, she would look upon us, mournfully.

The Spectre fully relished its hold over her. Its siren song called her toward the jagged shore where the destroyed souls of so many were recklessly strewn. There was only emptiness. Fear.

But then good news. *We caught it. It's all gone.* Triumphant news. But how could it be believed? We needed to believe.

It wasn't until several meetings with the surgeon and her team later that I truly understood that the threat had gone. I addressed the Spectre.

You no longer have power over me. I am not afraid. We will move forward. We are stronger now having faced you together.

The tight grip on my throat finally began to loosen. Part of me was lying, but I could never admit that.

The smile that had so long been absent graced her tired face. My mother returned, but she was changed. The damage was done, the Fear so complete. Rebuilding the hollowed part of her will take time, but for now we have time.

She spent her life protecting us, and we supported her during those dark and troubled times.

It was the one thing we were trained to do, and when it mattered, we did.

Transformed back into its wispy shadow self, the Spectre still hovers. As I sit on the train watching the icy water of Lake Ontario churn as I pass on my way to work, I can't help but think how much has happened in a year.

Tears gather in my eyes and I pull my sunglasses on. These tears are not for others.

For The Quiet

Abigail Grimes

Dear Briar

I know that we haven't spoken in a while, but I thought it would be best to have a bit of distance between us.

I thought it would help with the pain. I thought I could start to forget.

That was foolish and I apologize. You are part of me. You always will be. Recently, I was reminded of that.

I wonder if it is fair to feel a little bit sad even though you are happy.

Happiness is complicated. I don't think you can experience it, truly experience it, without knowing some element of sadness.

For The Quiet

*I heard some absolutely terrific news and
though I was so very happy to know it, a
part of me, the part of me that misses
you so desperately, couldn't help but
ache.*

*I am struggling with the guilt and I hope you
don't think any less of me for it.
I will speak with you again soon.*

*But in the interim, I will fully embrace the
happiness that surrounds me.*

Yours. Always.

Me

Abigail Grimes

And Here We Are

How many times have I ended a thought with
And here we are

I miss you today

I said your whole name out loud for the first
   time in nearly a year and it hurt so bad.

I sat for a long time,
crying,
feeling sorry for me, and for you

No one will ever know you

For The Quiet

That is one of my greatest regrets

And here we are
In this place where I can't forgive

And I won't forget.

Abigail Grimes

My Dearest Briar

I send you happiest wishes for this new year.

Being here, without you, has been difficult. Far more difficult than I could have ever imagined.

It is in this – emptiness – that I have had the time to reflect. To make peace. To find strength. But there is nothing here. Nothing but the pain, the regret, of a love lost.

I awoke from a dream. It was troubling and beautiful. It saddened me to know that wherever you are, you may be alone. But I was hopeful that you were at least happy.

Time has elapsed so quickly. Days to night, weeks and seasons. Decisions made and actions taken.

For The Quiet

All that is left is nothing.

I write this into the void. This I know. But I hope that one day, it will serve us both well.

With an aching heart and most sincere wishes for peace and love,

Me

Acknowledgements

൘ൡ

Writing the stories and the poems in this collection was extremely personal and at times very difficult. I know this collection wouldn't be possible if not for my amazing support system of family and friends.

Thank you to Odelia Oswago and Clancy Dias. You were subjected to numerous late-night messages because you so kindly offered to assist with my graphic design questions. Sorry, and thanks!

I would like to thank Anil Kamal for your patience and compassion when editing this book. Thank you for being an ear during the writing process and for taking the care these stories and poems needed, and as always, for your friendship.

Thank you to Cherlin McColman and Vanessa George for your love and sisterhood during some difficult times. You are always a sounding board and a reality check when I need one.

To my husband. This road has certainly been a challenging one. We are in it together and I am very grateful for you.

Last, but never least, to my daughter, Briar Elizabeth. From the moment I saw *Sleeping Beauty* as a child, I had decided upon your name. You exist only in my heart and mind and have resided there longer than any other dream. Though it may not be evident to anyone else, everything I do, I do to make you proud. I have written to you countless times over the years and doing so brings me immeasurable peace. You are home to me.

About the Author

☙❧

Abigail Grimes is the author of stories that range from bone-tingling thrillers and gripping fiction to poetry and non-fiction with heart.

She is the author of "The Violence of Fire" which is currently available wherever you buy books.

She works in the bustling metropolitan city of Toronto, Ontario and loves to write and relax at her home in rural Ontario, where she lives with her husband.

www.abigailgrimes.com

www.ingramcontent.com/pod-product-compliance
Lightning Source LLC
Chambersburg PA
CBHW020037120526
44589CB00032B/592